REAL REVOLUTIONARIES

THE REAL THOMAS JEFFERSON

THE TRUTH BEHIND THE LEGEND

by Eric Braun

COMPASS POINT BOOKS
a capstone imprint

Real Revolutionaries is published by Compass Point Books,
1710 Roe Crest Drive, North Mankato, Minnesota 56003
capstonepub.com

Library of Congress Cataloging-in-Publication Data is on file with the Library of Congress.
Names: Braun, Eric, 1971– author.
Title: The real Thomas Jefferson : the truth behind the legend / by Eric Braun.
Description: North Mankato, Minnesota : Compass Point Books, [2019] | Series: CPB grades 4-8. Real revolutionaries | Audience: Ages 10-14.
Identifiers: LCCN 2018042074| ISBN 9780756558918 (hardcover) | ISBN 9780756561277 (pbk.) | ISBN 9780756558963 (ebook pdf)
Subjects: LCSH: Jefferson, Thomas, 1743-1826—Juvenile literature. | Presidents—United States—Biography—Juvenile literature.
Classification: LCC E332.79 .B73 2019 | DDC 973.4/6092 [B]—dc23
LC record available at https://lccn.loc.gov/2018042074

Editorial Credits
Nick Healy, editor; Sarah Bennett, designer; Eric Gohl, media researcher; Kathy McColley, production specialist

Photo Credits
Alamy: LOC Photo, cover, 1; Bridgeman Images: Massachusetts Historical Society, Boston, MA, USA/Jefferson, Thomas (1743-1826), 49, National Geographic Image Collection/Silverfish Press/ National Geographic Creative/Meltzoff, Stanley (1917-2006), 51, Roger-Viollet, Paris/Musee Franco-Americaine, Blerancourt, Chauny, France/Jefferson, Thomas (1743-1826), 44; Getty Images: Stringer/Three Lions, 39; Granger: 13, 28, 41; Library of Congress: 6, 8; Newscom: CQ Roll Call Photos/Tom Williams, 34, Picture History, 20–21, UPI/Pat Benic, 53; North Wind Picture Archives: 17, 31, 57; Wikimedia: Public Domain, 23, 24–25

Design Elements
Shutterstock

Printed in the United States 6069

Contents

CHAPTER ONE

AN ACCOMPLISHED LIFE

In the Declaration of Independence, Thomas Jefferson wrote that "all men are created equal," an idea that has come to symbolize the very core of the United States of America. He not only wrote the Declaration, he served his country in many ways in its early years, from secretary of state to president. He is one of the most beloved of the American founding fathers. His most important achievements continue to shape the lives of Americans today.

AUTHOR OF THE DECLARATION OF INDEPENDENCE

It was late spring in 1776, and American colonists were getting fed up. For years they had enjoyed a good relationship with their mother country, Great Britain. Great Britain bought tobacco, cotton, wheat, and other crops from the colonies. And Britain helped protect the colonies from attack by other Europeans or American Indians. In return, the colonists bought nearly all their goods from Great Britain. They obeyed British laws and paid taxes to the British government.

Everything worked well for many years after the colonies were established, beginning with the first colony of Virginia in 1607. But by 1776, Great Britain was in trouble. The country was spending too much money on a long war with France. The British government increased taxes on the colonies to raise money. When some colonists complained, Great Britain cracked down. Britain's leaders refused to lower the taxes. They also sent more troops to the colonies to prevent rebellion. This, of course, made many colonists angry. More and more people started talking about independence.

By May 1776, eight of the 13 colonies supported independence from Great Britain. In June, leaders from all 13 colonies discussed the issue at the Second Continental Congress in Philadelphia. On June 7, Richard Henry Lee from Virginia made the first call for independence. Not everyone supported the idea. But the Congress selected a Committee of Five to write a document stating their reasons for demanding independence. The committee included John Adams of Massachusetts, Roger Sherman of Connecticut, Benjamin Franklin of Pennsylvania, and Robert R. Livingston of New York. It also included Thomas Jefferson of Virginia.

Jefferson was the only southerner on the Committee of Five. He was also younger than most of the others, but he was known as a talented writer. The committee selected him to write the first draft of the Declaration of

Benjamin Franklin (left) and John Adams (center) reviewed Jefferson's (right) draft and helped him shape the Declaration of Independence.

Independence. Jefferson didn't want to write it. He asked John Adams to do it. In a letter to a friend, Adams later described how he convinced Jefferson to undertake the task. When Jefferson suggested Adams write it, Adams replied that this would not go over well with the people.

"I am obnoxious, suspected, and unpopular," Adams told his friend. But people liked Jefferson. Adams's final reason that Jefferson should write the document was simple. As he said, "You can write ten times better than I can."

Jefferson replied, "I will do as well as I can."

And so he sat at his desk in his rented rooms in Philadelphia and wrote the first draft of the Declaration of Independence. He included the reasons why the 13 colonies were declaring themselves independent. He also defined the "legal and natural" rights of people. These, he wrote, include "Life, Liberty and the pursuit of Happiness."

Once he had a first draft, Jefferson asked Adams and Franklin for feedback. He made some changes, and just 17 days later, on July 4th, the Congress approved the Declaration of Independence. They had already voted in favor of independence from Great Britain two days previously. The president of the Continental Congress, John Hancock, was the first to sign it. By August 2nd, all 56 colonial delegates had signed the document.

Over the next several weeks, copies of the Declaration were delivered throughout the colonies. It was printed in newspapers, and it was read aloud to soldiers in the Continental Army. The effect was that more people began to support the idea of independence—and revolution.

A CHAMPION FOR RELIGIOUS FREEDOM

Before Thomas Jefferson died, he wrote his own epitaph. In the words he wanted on his gravestone, he included the three things he was most proud of. Although he had been a lawyer and a legislator, a governor and a U.S. president, he didn't mention those things.

His list included two of his other well-known accomplishments: He had written the Declaration of Independence, one of the most important documents in world history. And he had founded the University of Virginia, which became one of the most admired colleges in the world. Those were indeed two important milestones in his life.

What was the third item he named? Jefferson included the fact that he had written the Virginia Statute for Religious Freedom. Today, few people have heard of this 1785 law. But there was a reason Jefferson was so proud of it. It was one of the first attempts in world history to grant people the freedom of religion.

Until then, nearly every country had a major religion. People who practiced that religion had more power and more rights than those who didn't. For instance, in many European countries, the Catholic Church was the major religion. People who were not Catholic were discriminated against. They often could not hold positions of power or own property. They enjoyed fewer rights.

In Great Britain in the 1700s, the state religion was the Anglican Church. British citizens had to obey its laws. They had to pay taxes to the church. So did people who lived in Britain's North American colonies. That included the Commonwealth of Virginia, where Jefferson was a legislator.

Jefferson strongly believed that Virginia had to change. He felt that citizens could not be truly free if they could not practice their religion of choice. He wrote, "It does me no injury for my neighbor to say that there are twenty gods or no god. It neither picks my pocket nor breaks my leg." And he felt that the government should not be connected to any church.

Jefferson got his chance to make this change in October 1776. The Virginia General Assembly asked him and four other men to review Virginia laws. Their job was to update the laws to reflect the values of the colony of Virginia. The goal was to alter the laws so they would reflect Virginia's independence from Britain. In all, Jefferson and the others rewrote 126 laws into new bills.

Virginia's General Assembly would have to vote on the bills before they could be law. The Assembly never passed most of them. But in 1786, it passed "Bill No. 82." This became the "Virginia Statute for Religious Freedom." The new law said that government had to be separated from church activities. And it made it illegal to discriminate against anyone based on their religion.

When his bill became law in Virginia, Jefferson was in France. By then, he was serving as U.S. minister to that country. He was so excited about the new law that he had it translated into French. That way those around him could learn of it.

The idea of separating church and state was shocking to most Europeans. But Jefferson's law laid the groundwork for the American culture of religious tolerance. And it was later included in the first amendment to the U.S. Constitution. It begins, "Congress shall make no law respecting an establishment of religion, or prohibiting the free exercise thereof . . ."

THE THIRD

On the morning of March 3, 1801, Thomas Jefferson left his rooms at a boardinghouse in Washington, D.C. He walked to the U.S. Capitol to give his inaugural address to Congress. It was going to be his first speech after being elected the country's third president.

Even before he arrived, Jefferson signaled that he was going to be a different kind of president. Both George Washington and John Adams had worn elegant suits for their inaugural speeches. They had been driven to the Capitol in horse-drawn carriages. But Jefferson wore simple clothes and walked to his destination.

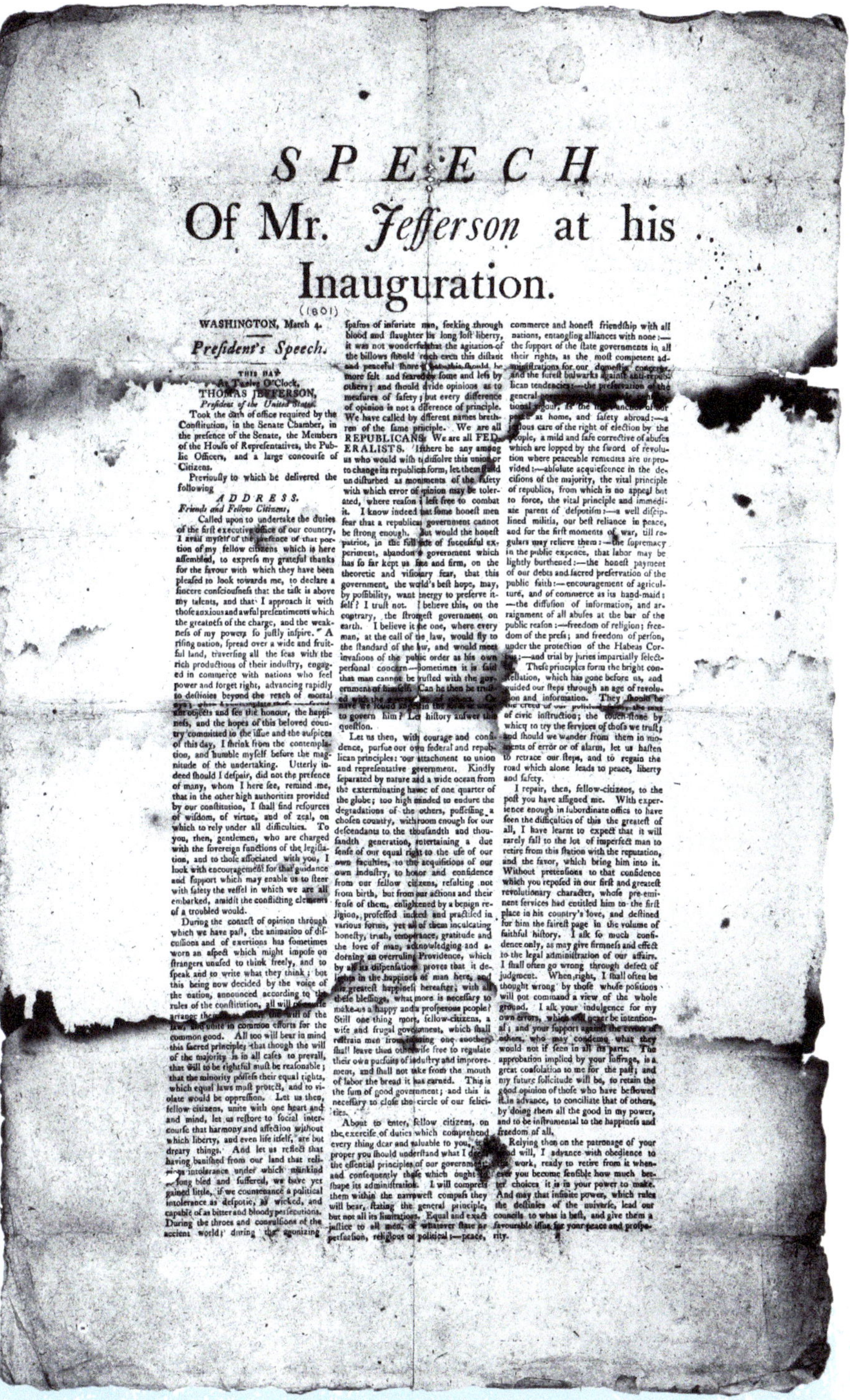

SPEECH Of Mr. *Jefferson* at his Inauguration.

(1801)

WASHINGTON, March 4.

Preſident's Speech.

THIS DAY

At Twelve O'Clock,

THOMAS JEFFERSON,

Preſident of the United States.

Took the oath of office required by the Conſtitution, in the Senate Chamber, in the preſence of the Senate, the Members of the Houſe of Repreſentatives, the Public Officers, and a large concourſe of Citizens.

Previouſly to which he delivered the following

ADDRESS.

Friends and Fellow Citizens,

Called upon to undertake the duties of the firſt executive office of our country, I avail myſelf of the preſence of that portion of my fellow citizens which is here aſſembled, to expreſs my grateful thanks for the favour with which they have been pleaſed to look towards me, to declare a ſincere conſciouſneſs that the taſk is above my talents, and that I approach it with thoſe anxious and awful preſentiments which the greatneſs of the charge, and the weakneſs of my powers ſo juſtly inſpire. A riſing nation, ſpread over a wide and fruitful land, traverſing all the ſeas with the rich productions of their induſtry, engaged in commerce with nations who feel power and forget right, advancing rapidly to deſtinies beyond the reach of mortal eye; [illegible] objects and ſee the honour, the happineſs, and the hopes of this beloved country committed to the iſſue and the auſpices of this day, I ſhrink from the contemplation, and humble myſelf before the magnitude of the undertaking. Utterly indeed ſhould I deſpair, did not the preſence of many, whom I here ſee, remind me, that in the other high authorities provided by our conſtitution, I ſhall find reſources of wiſdom, of virtue, and of zeal, on which to rely under all difficulties. To you, then, gentlemen, who are charged with the ſovereign functions of the legiſlation, and to thoſe aſſociated with you, I look with encouragement for that guidance and ſupport which may enable us to ſteer with ſafety the veſſel in which we are all embarked, amidſt the conflicting elements of a troubled would.

During the conteſt of opinion through which we have paſt, the animation of diſcuſſions and of exertions has ſometimes worn an aſpect which might impoſe on ſtrangers unuſed to think freely, and to ſpeak and to write what they think; but this being now decided by the voice of the nation, announced according to the rules of the conſtitution, all will of courſe arrange [illegible] the will of the law, and unite in common efforts for the common good. All too will bear in mind this ſacred principle, that though the will of the majority is in all caſes to prevail, that will to be rightful muſt be reaſonable; that the minority poſſeſs their equal rights, which equal laws muſt protect, and to violate would be oppreſſion. Let us then, fellow citizens, unite with one heart and and mind, let us reſtore to ſocial intercourſe that harmony and affection without which liberty, and even life itſelf, are but dreary things. And let us reflect that having baniſhed from our land that religious intolerance under which mankind ſo long bled and ſuffered, we have yet gained little, if we countenance a political intolerance as deſpotic, as wicked, and capable of as bitter and bloody perſecutions. During the throes and convulſions of the ancient world; during the agonizing ſpaſms of infuriate man, ſeeking through blood and ſlaughter his long loſt liberty, it was not wonderful that the agitation of the billows ſhould reach even this diſtant and peaceful ſhore; [illegible] ſhould be more felt and feared by ſome and leſs by others; and ſhould divide opinions as to meaſures of ſafety; but every difference of opinion is not a difference of principle. We have called by different names brethren of the ſame principle. We are all REPUBLICANS: We are all FEDERALISTS. If there be any among us who would wiſh to diſſolve this union or to change its republican form, let them ſtand undiſturbed as monuments of the ſafety with which error of opinion may be tolerated, where reaſon is left free to combat it. I know indeed that ſome honeſt men fear that a republican government cannot be ſtrong enough. But would the honeſt patriot, in the full tide of ſucceſsful experiment, abandon a government which has ſo far kept us free and firm, on the theoretic and viſionary fear, that this government, the world's beſt hope, may, by poſſibility, want energy to preſerve itſelf? I truſt not. I believe this, on the contrary, the ſtrongeſt government on earth. I believe it the one, where every man, at the call of the law, would fly to the ſtandard of the law, and would meet invaſions of the public order as his own perſonal concern.—Sometimes it is ſaid that man cannot be truſted with the government of himſelf. Can he then be truſted with the [illegible] Or have we found [illegible] to govern him? Let hiſtory anſwer this queſtion.

Let us then, with courage and confidence, purſue our own federal and republican principles: our attachment to union and repreſentative government. Kindly ſeparated by nature and a wide ocean from the exterminating havoc of one quarter of the globe; too high minded to endure the degradations of the others, poſſeſſing a choſen country, with room enough for our deſcendants to the thouſandth and thouſandth generation, entertaining a due ſenſe of our equal right to the uſe of our own faculties, to the acquiſitions of our own induſtry, to honor and confidence from our fellow citizens, reſulting not from birth, but from our actions and their ſenſe of them, enlightened by a benign religion, profeſſed indeed and practiſed in various forms, yet all of them inculcating honeſty, truth, temperance, gratitude and the love of man, acknowledging and adoring an overruling Providence, which by all its diſpenſations proves that it delights in the happineſs of man here, and his greateſt happineſs hereafter; with all theſe bleſſings, what more is neceſſary to make us a happy and a proſperous people? Still one thing more, fellow-citizens, a wiſe and frugal government, which ſhall reſtrain men from injuring one another, ſhall leave them otherwiſe free to regulate their own purſuits of induſtry and improvement, and ſhall not take from the mouth of labor the bread it has earned. This is the ſum of good government; and this is neceſſary to cloſe the circle of our felicities.

About to enter, fellow citizens, on the exerciſe of duties which comprehend every thing dear and valuable to you, it is proper you ſhould underſtand what I deem the eſſential principles of our government, and conſequently thoſe which ought to ſhape its adminiſtration. I will compreſs them within the narroweſt compaſs they will bear, ſtating the general principle, but not all its limitations. Equal and exact juſtice to all men, of whatever ſtate or perſuaſion, religious or political;—peace, commerce and honeſt friendſhip with all nations, entangling alliances with none:—the ſupport of the ſtate governments in all their rights, as the moſt competent adminiſtrations for our domeſtic concerns, and the fureſt bulwarks againſt anti-republican tendencies:—the preſervation of the general [illegible] tional vigour, as the [illegible] of our peace at home, and ſafety abroad:—a jealous care of the right of election by the people, a mild and ſafe corrective of abuſes which are lopped by the ſword of revolution where peaceable remedies are unprovided:—abſolute acquieſcence in the deciſions of the majority, the vital principle of republics, from which is no appeal but to force, the vital principle and immediate parent of deſpotiſm:—a well diſciplined militia, our beſt reliance in peace, and for the firſt moments of war, till regulars may relieve them:—the ſupremacy in the public expence, that labor may be lightly burthened:—the honeſt payment of our debts and ſacred preſervation of the public faith:—encouragement of agriculture, and of commerce as its hand-maid:—the diffuſion of information, and arraignment of all abuſes at the bar of the public reaſon:—freedom of religion; freedom of the preſs; and freedom of perſon, under the protection of the Habeas Corpus:—and trial by juries impartially ſelected. Theſe principles form the bright conſtellation, which has gone before us, and guided our ſteps through an age of revolution and information. They ſhould be the creed of our political [illegible] the text of civic inſtruction; the touch-ſtone by which to try the ſervices of thoſe we truſt; and ſhould we wander from them in moments of error or of alarm, let us haſten to retrace our ſteps, and to regain the road which alone leads to peace, liberty and ſafety.

I repair, then, fellow-citizens, to the poſt you have aſſigned me. With experience enough in ſubordinate offices to have ſeen the difficulties of this the greateſt of all, I have learnt to expect that it will rarely fall to the lot of imperfect man to retire from this ſtation with the reputation, and the favor, which bring him into it. Without pretenſions to that confidence which you repoſed in our firſt and greateſt revolutionary character, whoſe pre-eminent ſervices had entitled him to the firſt place in his country's love, and deſtined for him the faireſt page in the volume of faithful hiſtory. I aſk ſo much confidence only, as may give firmneſs and effect to the legal adminiſtration of our affairs. I ſhall often go wrong through defect of judgment. When right, I ſhall often be thought wrong by thoſe whoſe poſitions will not command a view of the whole ground. I aſk your indulgence for my own errors, which will never be intentional; and your ſupport againſt the errors of others, who may condemn what they would not if ſeen in all its parts. The approbation implied by your ſuffrage, is a great conſolation to me for the paſt; and my future ſolicitude will be, to retain the good opinion of thoſe who have beſtowed it in advance, to conciliate that of others, by doing them all the good in my power, and to be inſtrumental to the happineſs and freedom of all.

Relying then on the patronage of your good will, I advance with obedience to the work, ready to retire from it whenever you become ſenſible how much better choices it is in your power to make. And may that infinite power, which rules the deſtinies of the univerſe, lead our councils to what is beſt, and give them a favourable iſſue for your peace and proſperity.

Jefferson used his inaugural address to call on Americans to unite around their shared ideals.

Once in the crowded Capitol, he spoke softly and quietly. He laid out his plans for his presidency. He stressed that the most important task for the American people was to unite behind their government. The country should "unite with one heart and one mind," he said. He had good reason to highlight the importance of unity. The nation had been greatly divided during his election.

Jefferson had first run for president against John Adams in 1796 and lost a close election. At the time, the person with the second-most votes became vice president. That was Jefferson's fate. Adams became the second U.S. president, and Jefferson was his vice president.

In the next election, in 1800, Jefferson ran against Adams again. And although the two had worked together as president and vice president, the election was bitter. Adams was a Federalist. He and his party believed in a strong central government. Jefferson was a Democratic-Republican. He and his party believed in strong state and local governments. Jefferson's supporters said Adams wanted to be a king, not a president. And Adams's supporters said Jefferson didn't believe in God. Jefferson once said that, during the election, newspapers were full of "every falsehood they can invent."

An unexpected thing happened when the Electoral College votes were counted in early December 1800. Jefferson beat Adams, but he tied with another member of his own Democratic-Republican Party named Aaron Burr. That meant the U.S. House of Representatives would hold a tie-breaking vote. So in February 1801, the House met and took up the matter. Jefferson and Burr were both Democratic-Republicans, but members of that party were united in voting for Jefferson. Their intention all along had been to elect him to the top job and Burr to the lesser role.

Members of Adams's Federalist Party, however, did not want Jefferson to become president. They voted for Burr instead. The first House vote ended in a tie. It took 36 votes spread over seven days until a winner emerged.

In calling for Americans to be united, Jefferson said that all of us are "brethren of the same principle. We are all Republicans, we are all Federalists."

Adams had left town in the middle of the night. But others heard Jefferson's message and took it to heart. The election had been vicious, yet the transfer of power was peaceful. This was not common in the world at that time.

Jefferson was inaugurated as the third president on March 4, 1801. He would serve two terms in the role.

EXPANDING THE UNITED STATES

When Jefferson became president, the United States included 16 states and a total of about 800,000 square miles (2,072,000 square kilometers) of land. Within his first two years in office, Ohio became the 17th state. The new state was full of fertile farmland—as were the states of Pennsylvania, West Virginia, and Virginia.

Fertile farmland was a boon to the country, but there was a problem. Those farmers needed access to the Mississippi River and the Gulf of Mexico. Without it, they couldn't export their crops and make money. But the United States didn't own the land through which the Mississippi flowed. France did.

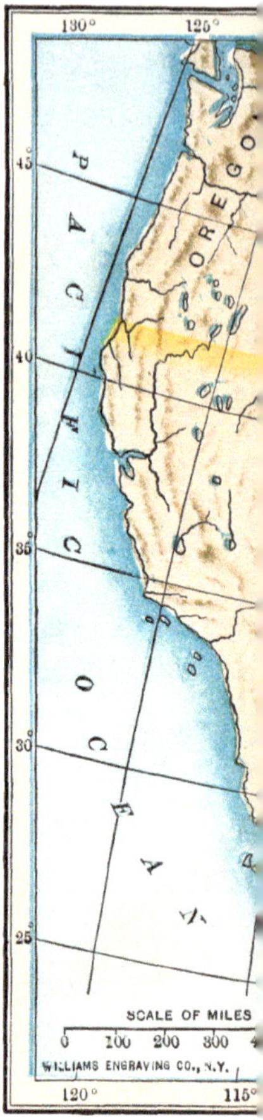

The area was called Louisiana, and it included the large port city of New Orleans. The city was valuable because it controlled trade in and out of the entire region.

Jefferson wanted to buy the city of New Orleans from the French. He thought it would be hard to convince them to sell. But he got lucky—French leader Napoleon Bonaparte needed money to support his war with Great Britain. He offered to sell not just the city of New Orleans, but the whole Louisiana territory. And he offered to sell it for the bargain price of $15 million.

Jefferson was satisfied with the deal. The United States would add 830,000 square miles (2,150,000 square km) for a low price. But the president was worried about overstepping his powers. After all, as a Democratic-Republican he believed in limiting the role of the president. He believed the federal government should only take actions that were specifically allowed in the U.S. Constitution. Buying new land was not on that list.

The Louisiana Purchase amounted to a massive expansion of U.S. territory.

He thought about seeking an amendment—a permanent change—to the Constitution. But that would take time to make official, and Napoleon was getting impatient. He wanted his money soon.

So Jefferson ignored his concerns about the Constitution. He asked Congress to approve the deal for buying the new land. Lawmakers approved it in October 1803. On December 20th, the French flag was lowered in New Orleans, and the American flag was raised. The United States had just doubled in size.

The Louisiana Purchase delivered huge benefits to the United Sates. It helped American farmers and traders to flourish. But it caused political problems for the president. His enemies called him a hypocrite. In pushing the deal through Congress, he had done just what he often accused the Federalists of doing. He had overstepped the rights of the states.

The Louisiana Purchase offered great new opportunities to the United States. Even before that, many Americans were fascinated by the unsettled lands west of the Mississippi River. President Jefferson was particularly interested in the undiscovered plant and animal life of the West. He also wanted to find a path to the Pacific Ocean so Americans could trade goods directly with Asia. Jefferson sent an expedition to the Pacific Northwest. He selected Meriwether Lewis and William Clark to lead the expedition. Lewis was Jefferson's personal secretary, but he was made an army officer for the assignment. He was not yet 30 years old, but he had already explored the West many times.

Jefferson asked Lewis and Clark to find a good route to the Pacific Ocean. He told them to explore trading with the American Indians they met on the way. He also asked them to study the geography, plants, and animals of the area. They set off from St. Louis in May 1804. They traveled through the Dakotas and over the Rocky Mountains. They found the Columbia River and followed it to the Pacific Ocean.

Sixteen months later, they returned to St. Louis. They had mapped out a trade route. They had collected samples of new plants and animals. The West was no longer the great unknown. Organizing the Lewis and Clark expedition would go down in history as another of Jefferson's biggest accomplishments.

CHAMPION FOR EDUCATION

After his presidency was over, Jefferson could have spent his later years relaxing. Instead, he traveled almost every day from his home to a construction site. The 4-mile (6.4-km) horse ride in all kinds of weather was not always easy for a man in his mid-60s. His days at the site were probably difficult. But this was important to him. He was overseeing construction of the University of Virginia.

In the Declaration of Independence, Jefferson didn't only write about people's rights to life, liberty, and the pursuit of happiness. He also said they should have a say in their government. In fact, American citizens were given a duty to participate in government by voting. And to be able to do that, Jefferson believed, people needed an education. Without it, people wouldn't fully understand their duties and rights.

In Jefferson's time, only wealthy people could attend school. He knew that if only wealthy people were educated, then only wealthy people would control the government. He wanted all people to get an education.

Jefferson worked his whole life to make education available to more people. In 1779, he was a member of the Virginia House of Delegates. There, he wrote his ideas into a bill. The bill was called "A Bill for the More General Diffusion of Knowledge." It called for Virginia to have public schools that children would attend for free. The schools would teach reading, writing, math, and history. And he called for at least one free school every 5 to 6 square miles (13 to 16 square km) so that they would be accessible to every child. The House of Delegates did not pass his bill. But Jefferson had gotten his ideas about free education into the public mind.

Years later, after his time as president, Jefferson came back to his interest in education. This time he focused on educating young adults rather than children. But the main idea was the same. He wanted the general public to have access to quality education.

At the time, most colleges and universities were tied to a religion or church. Most graduates became preachers or professors. Jefferson wanted to educate future business and political leaders. He wanted the university, not a church, to decide what courses would be offered. And he wanted students to have many subjects to choose from. He decided to create such a university in his home state of Virginia.

Among Jefferson's many personal interests was a love of architecture. He had designed both his home estate of Monticello and the Virginia State Capitol in Richmond. Now he helped design the campus for the new University of Virginia in Charlottesville. And he rode there every day to watch over progress on the construction. Jefferson paid attention to every detail. He even determined how loud the bell should ring.

He based the architecture on ancient Roman ruins. The university was made up of many buildings. At that

The University of Virginia's campus was built to suit Jefferson's vision.

time, other such institutions were each housed in one large building. Jefferson's new design became the model for modern universities. A surprising highlight of his design was that the entire university was centered around a library. Most universities were centered around a church.

The University of Virginia's first classes started in March 1825. True to Jefferson's ideas, it offered a wide variety of subjects. Students could study math and history. But they could also study botany, astronomy, and architecture. One subject that was not taught: religion.

CHAPTER TWO

JEFFERSON IN LEGEND AND MYTH

Because Jefferson is such an important figure in history, many stories have been told about him—not all of which are true. While he was undoubtedly a very important figure in American history, some stories show him in an idealized light, ignoring his faults or exaggerating his greatness.

A LEADER FOR ALL PEOPLE?

Thomas Jefferson may be most well known for the following words. He wrote them in the Declaration of Independence.

All men are created equal.

All his life, Jefferson worked to advance the rights of common people. He fought for people's rights to education. He fought for their rights to practice the religion of their choice. But did he really believe that everyone was created equal?

The answer is: not exactly.

There are several examples from Jefferson's words and actions that show he did not consider women to be equal to men. He also didn't believe American Indians or African Americans were equal to white men. He was not alone in thinking that way. Most white men of his time believed they were superior to other people.

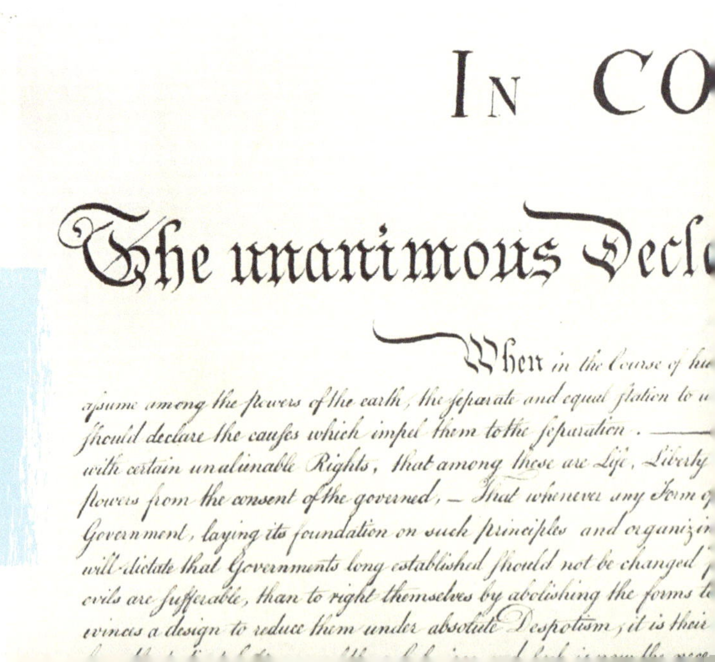

Jefferson's words proclaimed equality among all men, but his actions reflected clear inequalities.

Jefferson, however, had more respect for American Indians than most of his contemporaries. From the time Europeans first arrived in North America, they had treated the native people poorly. Many Europeans falsely claimed it was a scientific fact that American Indians were inferior to them. Some said the difference was caused by the climate and geography of North America. Jefferson was one of the first white people to stand up against this idea. In 1785, he wrote, "I believe the Indian then to be in body and mind equal to the whiteman."

Yet he also wrote that he believed American Indians' culture caused its people to be inferior. He later wrote that they should give up their lifestyle of hunting and village life. They should adopt European customs of farming and living in cities and towns. Then they would become civilized. As president, Jefferson backed policies that encouraged American Indian tribes to give up their

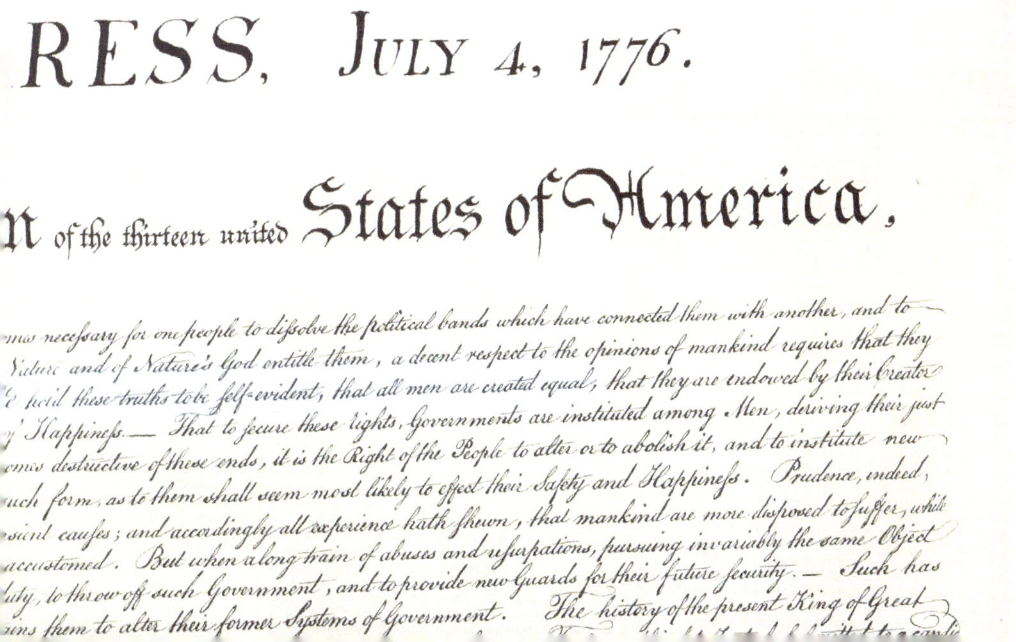

traditional lifestyle—and their land. Instead, they would settle in American cities and towns.

Jefferson's thoughts on African Americans were also complicated. As president, he signed a law ending the slave trade. After January 1, 1808, it was illegal to bring new slaves to the United States. This was one of the most important things he did. He saw it as a first step to ending slavery in the United States.

A slaveholder himself, President Jefferson said he wanted to end slavery altogether in the United States. But he believed it had to happen gradually. Outlawing the slave trade was the first step. Next, he said, slave owners would treat enslaved people better. This would improve slavery, he believed. The next step would be that all enslaved people born after a certain date would be freed. And the final step would be making all slavery illegal.

Of course, it did not work out that way. During Jefferson's lifetime, slavery only grew stronger in some ways. And slavery in the United States would endure for more than 50 years after Jefferson's presidency—long after he and his peers were gone—and would nearly tear the country apart.

He continued to work to end it. But even so, he did not believe that freed slaves could live as equals among white Americans. He did believe that enslaved people had the right to personal liberty and freedom. But he also believed that black people were inferior to white people and "as incapable as children." Jefferson, along with many others who worked to end slavery in the early 1800s, believed that, once freed, former slaves should be sent back to Africa to live.

A SUCCESSFUL PRESIDENT?

Nearly everyone agrees: Thomas Jefferson was an excellent president. In the 2017 Presidential Historian Survey, experts in U.S. history ranked him the seventh-best president of all time.

But was he a complete success as president? The short answer is no.

He was better at some things than others. In the survey, historians gave him the highest marks in three areas. They are his overall vision, his moral authority, and his relationship with Congress. But they gave him lower ratings for "crisis leadership" and "economic management."

To see why, take a look at his actions with foreign trade. Trading goods with other countries is a key part of any nation's success. It's nearly impossible for a country to be self-sufficient. Countries can't grow and produce everything that citizens need—and only as much as they need. Instead, most countries specialize in certain goods. They grow or produce more than they need. Then they sell (export) those goods to other countries. They buy (import) other goods that their own citizens need. The trick is to maintain a balance. That way a country doesn't become poor by importing more than it exports.

In the early 1800s, the United States traded goods with many European countries. But the Napoleonic Wars started in 1803, and the fight between France and Great Britain caused a big problem for Americans. Naval battles interrupted trade between those countries and the United States. Both the French and British forces attacked American trade ships.

Americans were angry at the British for another reason too. Great Britain was kidnapping Americans and forcing them into the British Navy. During the war, many British sailors had deserted the British Navy. To escape war, they joined American merchant marine ships.

An early political cartoon reflected a dim view of Jefferson in comparison to George Washington. On the left, Washington is shown beneath rays of sunshine, whereas Jefferson is shown under a dark cloud.

These boats carried goods for trade to and from Europe. So the British Navy began raiding American ships. They would haul away anyone they thought was a British deserter. But they also hauled away many American sailors. They forced them to join the British Navy. Some people estimated that they kidnapped nine American sailors for every British deserter they caught.

Jefferson argued with Britain for several years. But the British Navy did not stop raiding American ships. So Jefferson and the U.S. Congress decided to punish Britain. One way to do that was to limit the goods they sold to Britain. In 1807, Congress passed—and President Jefferson signed—the Embargo Act. The law outlawed all trade between the United States and all other countries.

Jefferson hoped that the Embargo Act would hurt Britain. They would need American goods so badly that they would change their actions. They would treat the United States better.

But Great Britain did not suffer as he hoped. The British found other countries to import goods from. The United States suffered much more. Americans lost money because they couldn't sell their goods internationally.

The Embargo Act was ended in 1809, but the American economy suffered for years after. It was a low point in U.S. history. The Embargo Act became a symbol of Jefferson's weakness in handling a crisis and managing the economy.

A WHITE HOUSE EXECUTION?

In 2001, a movie called *Swordfish* was released. In it, a character says, "Thomas Jefferson once shot a man on the White House lawn for treason." History buffs who saw or heard about the film were surprised and confused. This was information that no one had heard before.

Soon after the film was released, people began searching for any truth behind the claim. Internet discussions lit up with questions about the incident. A person claiming to be a history professor named Robert Ludlum confirmed the story in a Yahoo! Answers post. He told a dramatic story that took place during Jefferson's presidential campaign. According to Ludlum, a North Carolina man named Rodney Cox had been giving away U.S. Navy secrets to the British. Ludlum said that Jefferson shot Cox himself. "It took 10 hours for Cox to expire," Ludlum wrote. While Cox died, "He lay prostrate on the White House lawn."

It turns out there was a good reason people hadn't heard this story before—it never happened. Historians researched the victim, Rodney Cox, and found that he never existed. They also researched Professor Robert Ludlum and found that there was no history professor with that name. Experts at the Thomas Jefferson Foundation issued a final ruling on the myth. "We have no evidence that this event ever occurred," they said. "No such thing is ever mentioned in Jefferson's papers, or contemporary newspaper accounts."

The deadly duel between Aaron Burr and Alexander Hamilton is a bit of real history, unlike the myth of Jefferson as executioner.

Experts on Thomas Jefferson were not sure how the myth came to be. Perhaps someone misremembered the famous duel between Aaron Burr and Alexander Hamilton. The duel, during which Burr mortally wounded Hamilton, was in 1804, while Jefferson was president. Still, the duel happened in New Jersey—not exactly the White House lawn.

There is another possible source of the myth. In 1778, Jefferson was a member of the Virginia legislature. That year he ordered the execution of an outlaw named Josiah Philips. Philips was a criminal, a murderer, and terrorist. He was also sympathetic to the British. Not only that, he had also been accused of stealing 28 hats and 5 pounds (2.3 kilograms) of twine.

In those days—before the U.S. Constitution made it illegal—the government could accuse someone of a crime and sentence him to death without even holding a trial. That's what happened to Philips. Jefferson and other lawmakers saw Philips as a threat to security. They had him hunted out of his hideout in the Great Dismal Swamp in southern Virginia. And then he was hanged.

There's no evidence that Jefferson executed a traitor on the White House lawn. He did have a hand in the execution of Josiah Philips. That he did so without a trial is shocking when thinking about Jefferson. He was famous for his insistence that everyone had rights.

Shocking or not, it is not the same as killing a man on the White House lawn. That story is a myth.

THE BIBLE, BY THOMAS JEFFERSON?

Imagine former president Thomas Jefferson sitting up late by lamp light. He has a razor, and carefully cut scraps of paper lie scattered all around. In one hand is a copy of the Bible. He is involved in a wild project. He's cutting up the pages and getting rid of the parts he doesn't like. The parts he does like, he pastes back together on a big board.

This story is true, though over the years it has turned into the myth that Thomas Jefferson wrote his own Bible. Not exactly. What Jefferson did was create his own pasted-together version of the Bible.

It was an 84-page book he called *The Life and Morals of Jesus of Nazareth*. Many people now refer to it as "Jefferson's Bible."

Jefferson started with several copies of the New Testament. He didn't agree with much of anything from the Old Testament, so he left it out completely. He had bibles in four different languages: English, Latin, French, and Greek. After all, Jefferson could read and write in six languages. Mostly he removed parts he didn't agree with and kept parts he did.

What did he leave out? Jefferson left out the parts that he thought could not have really happened. He didn't believe in miracles or the supernatural. So he cut out stories of Jesus performing miracles. For instance, the Bible includes a story of Jesus feeding a large crowd with just two fish and five loaves of bread. That story didn't make the cut for Jefferson's book. Sometimes he even cut stories in half. For instance, one Bible verse includes Jesus telling people not to work on the Sabbath. It also includes a story of a miraculous healing. Jefferson kept the advice about not working on the Sabbath, but he clipped out the magical part.

Jefferson had complex beliefs about religion. He believed that there was a God who had created the world. But he also believed in science. He thought the world was controlled by the rules of science. He didn't believe that God continued to control everything that happened in the world.

Jefferson believed that Jesus was a real person, but not a divine person. That is, he didn't believe Jesus was a god or that he could perform miracles. So in Jefferson's book, Jesus is a wise teacher. He gives advice on right and wrong. But he doesn't do anything that is scientifically impossible.

Jefferson's religious beliefs caused him some trouble in politics. Some people claimed that he wasn't a Christian. During his presidential election, critics accused him of not believing in God. This was hurtful to Jefferson. He believed in God. He just didn't believe the miraculous stories in the Bible.

Jefferson was interested in the Bible for most of his life. He studied it in depth. He began creating his own version of the New Testament in 1804. Jefferson was still president at the time. He put the project away for several years and went back to it around 1815.

Jefferson spent several years cutting out Bible parts in different languages. He wanted to compare how it was the same and how it was different in different languages. So he took a piece of paper and drew a huge table with four columns. He had one column for each language, and he glued down his scraps of paper on the columns. Once he decided which columns he liked best, he collected those into one 84-page book.

It seems he completed *The Life and Morals of Jesus of Nazareth* by 1820. It was published after Jefferson's death in 1826.

Jefferson pieced together a version of the Bible that was devoted to the words and deeds of Jesus Christ, leaving out accounts of miracles performed by him.

CHAPTER THREE

THE UNKNOWN JEFFERSON

Most people know that Thomas Jefferson wrote the Declaration of Independence and served as the third president of the United States. But Jefferson's impact on history goes deeper than that. He worked to increase education and ensure that the power in American government was truly in the hands of the people.

LIMITING GOVERNMENT

One complained that the other would not stop talking. The other one accused the first one of laughing and smirking across the table. Does that sound like two children? Actually, it was two grown men—leaders of the new nation, the United States.

Thomas Jefferson and Alexander Hamilton were selected by President George Washington to be part of the country's first government. Hamilton was secretary of the treasury. Jefferson was secretary of state. In those roles, they would work closely together. But the two men had nearly opposite personalities.

Jefferson was a quiet man. He preferred to think things through and write down his ideas. He was one of the most educated Americans of his time. Hamilton was talkative. He liked to argue with people who disagreed with him. Jefferson thought he was a bully. Hamilton thought Jefferson was sneaky and snobby. It would soon be obvious that the two would not work well together.

Jefferson was well qualified for the job of secretary of state. He had already served as minister to France from 1784 to 1789. He had lived in France and represented the U.S. government there. As a diplomat, he supported France in its war against Great Britain. He left France just as the French Revolution was breaking out. In that uprising of French citizens against their monarchy, Jefferson supported the ordinary citizens.

Jefferson planned to leave government work when he returned home in 1789. Instead, he agreed to serve as President Washington's secretary of state. Among other things, he was in charge of foreign affairs—how the government would work with other countries. That meant that on some issues he would work with Hamilton. As secretary of the treasury, Hamilton was in charge of issues having to do with money and banking.

One important issue that Jefferson and Hamilton worked on together was how to repay the country's war debts. During the Revolutionary War, states had taken out large loans from European countries. They needed money to pay for war costs. Now it was time to pay back the loans.

Jefferson believed each state should pay its own debt. He thought that was fair because some states owed more money than other states. But Hamilton believed that the states should add all their debts together. He thought the federal government should collect taxes from every citizen and pay all of the debts. After all, the states had been fighting together and toward the same goal. And, overall, Hamilton believed in a strong central government. Because of this he was called a Federalist.

Jefferson argued that a strong central government would take power away from the people. He thought it would be too close to the British monarchy. He accused Hamilton of wanting to create another monarchy in the United States. He even accused Hamilton of secretly working for Great Britain. (Meanwhile, Hamilton accused Jefferson of loving France more than he loved his own country.)

At the time, Jefferson's views were called Democratic-Republican. He believed that the federal government should only have power that the Constitution specifically gives it. Anything beyond that, he argued, took rights away from the common people.

The Democratic-Republican Party of Jefferson's day changed many times before it became today's Republican Party. But the belief in a limited central government remains strong. For this reason, some people call Jefferson the father of the Republican Party.

Both Jefferson (left) and Alexander Hamilton (center) were members of President George Washington's (right) cabinet, but they were not allies.

Jefferson himself might disagree with that label. He might say that just as many of his views, such as his belief in free education and the rights of the common citizens, can be found in today's Democratic Party.

FATHER OF AMERICAN ARCHAEOLOGY

In the countryside near Jefferson's home in Virginia lay an American Indian burial mound. When he was young, he saw a party of Indians visit the mound. (Jefferson may have been as young as eight, but historians aren't sure exactly how old he was.) The group left the main road nearby and traveled about 12 miles (19 km) through the woods. Then they arrived at the site. Jefferson wrote that they had "expressions which were construed to be those of sorrow."

The image of the American Indians grieving their ancestors must have made an impression on young Jefferson. All his life, he had a great interest in learning more about the tribes of Virginia. Later, in 1780, a French diplomat asked the Continental Congress questions about the 13 American states. Jefferson took on the job of answering the questions about Virginia.

One of the questions was about the native people who lived in the area that became Virginia. Jefferson researched them and wrote about their history and language. He also wrote about the land where they had lived. And he wrote about the burial mound.

A mill at Shadwell, Virginia, where Jefferson was born

The mound was located near the Rivanna River. Across the river, on some nearby hills, there had been what Jefferson called an "Indian town." This was later identified by scholars as a village of the Monacan Indians.

To learn as much as he could about the mound, Jefferson excavated it. This was a complicated process. First, he dug shallow holes into the surface. In these, he discovered human bones. He noted that the bones were "lying in the utmost confusion." The bones did not seem to be laid evenly or in a pattern. They came from multiple people. And they were not buried among any artifacts such as weapons or jewelry.

What Jefferson did next was radical. He cut a long, deep trench through the middle of the mound. A person could stand in the trench and look at the earth on either side. From that viewpoint, he could see layers, or strata, of earth. Each strata represented a different era of history. The bones nearest the surface were the least decayed. The bones lower down were more decayed. This showed that the mound had been used for several generations.

Jefferson also noted that the bones did not have any violent damage to them. They had no holes from bullets or arrows. Some people had thought the mound might have been only for warriors. But Jefferson's discovery showed that the dead buried there had not been in battles.

Jefferson wrote about his findings along with answers to all the other questions the French diplomat asked. His answers were thorough and detailed. They were later published as a book, *Notes on the State of Virginia*.

In his life, Jefferson wrote a lot. He made notes nearly every day on many topics, but he never meant to write a book about Virginia. Yet, historians later said *Notes* was the "most important scientific and political book written by an American before 1785."

Especially important was his writing on the burial mounds. His method of trenching and studying strata was unheard of. It would not be used by other archaeologists for another 100 years. But then it would become standard. Because of his innovations, Jefferson is known as the "Father of American Archaeology."

REVOLUTIONARY FARMER

Thomas Jefferson's home state of Virginia was farm country. The rich, fertile soil was perfect for growing crops. When the first Europeans arrived there in the 1500s, they began growing tobacco. They soon learned to grow corn from American Indians. The planters became wealthy selling their tobacco to Europe. They used their corn crops to feed themselves and their animals.

Few of those farmers thought about how they were affecting Virginia's soil. They didn't know how farming practices could help or hurt the land. They just kept growing the same two crops and using the same farming methods.

From a young age, Jefferson was interested in the natural world. He was fascinated by learning which plants grew best in different climates. He treated his gardens like a laboratory. He experimented with different species of plants and with different growing techniques. He studied natural sciences. In his life, Jefferson grew 170 different kinds of fruits and 330 types of vegetables. He kept careful records of when plants were planted, when they sprouted, and when they were harvested. He even knew exactly how many peas made up a pint.

Jefferson figured out that growing only corn and tobacco was damaging Virginia's farmland. By growing only the same two crops, the farmers were ruining the rich soil. And they were further harming the land by using poor farming methods.

To solve this, Jefferson introduced three key changes to Virginia farming. The first was crop rotation. He created a seven-year plan for growing different crops on the same land. He added some new crops to work into the crop rotation. He began growing potatoes, wheat, turnips, rye, and clover.

Changing the crops each year, or even each season, helps keep the soil in better shape. Each crop uses different nutrients from the soil instead of the same crop using up the same nutrients all the time. Rotation keeps the nutrients changing. By adding grasses and clover, Jefferson helped the soil bind together, so it was less likely to wash away in heavy rains. Adding grasses and clover helps the soil grow more and better crops over time.

The next big change Jefferson introduced was to add fertilizer to the soil. Adding a substance such as manure

Monticello was Jefferson's stately home, but it was also a large plantation where he experimented with processes to improve what his fields produced.

helps to nourish the soil. Soil needs that nourishment after it has produced crops for several years. At the time, Virginia farmers would keep growing the same crops on the same land until the soil just wouldn't grow those crops anymore. Then they moved on to new land. In the colonies, it sometimes seemed as if land was never-ending. As Jefferson once noted, "We can buy an acre of new land cheaper than we can manure an old acre."

But Jefferson knew that eventually people would run out of new land to farm. He made it his mission to change that practice. He used manure and other fertilizers. And he encouraged his fellow farmers to do the same. Then the same soil could be healthy and fruitful much longer.

The third big change that Jefferson brought to farming was a new way of plowing fields. Traditionally, farmers had used a plow that dug only 2 or 3 inches (5 to 8 centimeters) into the soil. And they plowed in straight up-and-down rows. Those two actions made the soil wash away quickly. The plow only loosened the very top layer of soil. And the straight crop lines left a path for the loose soil to wash away during heavy rains. Jefferson invented a new plow that dug down 6 inches (15 cm). He also began plowing in lines that followed the curves of the hills. Those two changes kept the soil from washing away.

Jefferson believed that the American people should live natural lives. They should be close to the land, and they should value it and conserve it. By advancing farming practices, he helped them do that.

CHAPTER FOUR

DIFFICULT TRUTHS

Although Thomas Jefferson is well known as being intelligent, thoughtful, and devoted to individual liberty, his story is more complicated than those words describe. To see a fuller picture, it's important to look at some of the darker parts of his life, starting with the end of it.

LIVING BEYOND HIS MEANS

Thomas Jefferson was an old man, and he was terribly anxious. He lay in bed worrying, tossing and turning and unable to sleep. As president, he had reduced the nation's debt—the money it owed to other countries. He was proud of that accomplishment. But he was not so successful in his personal finances.

By the end of his life, he and his family owed about $107,000 to banks and other creditors. Converted to a modern figure, that would be somewhere between $1 million to $2 million. The founding father faced the idea of dying and leaving his family with a massive financial burden to bear.

How had this happened? Many factors contributed to the problem. For one thing, it was sometimes hard to make money as a farmer. He had a lot of land and slaves. He could always feed and care for everyone at Monticello. But he could not always sell his goods and make money. When he did, he often did not get paid on time—or at all.

When Jefferson married Martha Wayles Skelton, he received a portion of her father's land and slaves. That wealth must have been welcomed by Jefferson, but when Martha's father died in 1774, Jefferson inherited his debts, which were large.

A few years after Jefferson retired from the presidency, the nation fought the War of 1812. At that time, it was hard for anyone to make money because resources were focused on the war effort. After the war, there was a recession. Banks didn't give out loans as easily, and few people were buying anything. This made it even harder for Jefferson to sell his goods. To make matters worse, he made some poor business decisions during this time. Soon the recession, also called the "Great Panic," plunged him deeper into debt.

Then there was more bad news. Around that time, a friend of Jefferson's came to him for financial help. He was desperate. Feeling obligated, Jefferson lent him $20,000.

But when the friend died in 1820, his estate was unable to pay Jefferson back. He had to take that $20,000 as a loss.

Jefferson tried to sell some land. But the value of land in Virginia was low at that time. Part of the reason was because of something Jefferson had done as president. The Louisiana Purchase had doubled the size of the United States. It also made new U.S. land in the West more interesting to buyers. Land in Virginia and other colonies decreased in value.

Some of these problems were beyond Jefferson's control. Others, like helping his friend, must have felt like the right thing to do. But some of his trouble was of his own making. Jefferson loved to live well. He spent lots of money on fancy furniture and wine. He undertook several building projects at Monticello that were expensive and ill advised. He tended to spend money on credit that he couldn't afford to repay.

That was why, as he was nearing the end of his life, he was so very anxious. He did not want to leave his family with large debts after he died. During one of those sleepless nights he came up with an idea to solve the problem—a lottery.

He figured that he could not make enough money by just selling his properties. The values were depressed after the war. But he could sell lots of lottery tickets. Many people would pay for the chance to win the property. But only one lucky winner would actually get it.

The lottery had not been conducted by the time Jefferson died on July 4, 1826. Afterward, one of his grandsons, Thomas Jefferson Randolph, tried to get the government to allow a lottery to help with Jefferson's debts. But it never happened. Monticello and 552 acres (223 hectares) of land were sold in 1831. Jefferson's slaves, other parcels of land, livestock, farming implements, and furniture were also sold. Even then, it wasn't enough to pay all the money Jefferson owed. Randolph was forced to take on his grandfather's debt.

One of Jefferson's early plans for his home at Monticello

ENSLAVING HUNDREDS

From the moment Thomas Jefferson was born, he was surrounded by enslaved people. Slaves put the newborn Thomas in his cradle. They helped raise him. As an adult, enslaved people helped run his home and grounds. When he married Martha Wayles Skelton in 1772, he doubled both his land and the number of enslaved people considered his property. And as he died, slaves stood by his side and comforted him.

Over the course of his life, Jefferson owned more than 600 enslaved people. That fact can be hard to reconcile with the idea of him as someone who dedicated his life to liberty. He wrote the Declaration of Independence. It said that "all men are created equal." He called slavery a violation of the natural rights of man. As president, he made it illegal to import slaves from other countries.

And yet, like most white Americans of his time, Jefferson held views that we now consider racist. He believed that black people were inferior to white people, both mentally and physically. And even though he thought slavery should end, he said that black people could not live alongside white people. If African Americans were freed, he said, they should return to Africa or Haiti. He did not think former slaves could live peacefully alongside their former masters.

Jefferson wrote, "We have the wolf by the ear, and we can neither hold him nor safely let him go. Justice is in one scale, and self-preservation in the other."

Jefferson utilized the work of enslaved people in almost every aspect of his life. They provided him with everything he needed.

One aspect of Jefferson's relationship with slavery has been much debated over the years. Back when Jefferson was running for reelection as president, a writer named James T. Callender wrote a newspaper story about him. Callender had been an ally of Jefferson. But the two had a falling out. To get revenge, Callender wrote that Jefferson was sexually involved with one of his slaves. Her name was Sally Hemings.

Jefferson's family and supporters denied the charge, though Jefferson did not respond publicly. But rumors persisted. Sally Hemings had several children that were light skinned. They looked like Jefferson. And over the years, evidence has piled up. It is almost certain that Jefferson was the father of several children born to Hemings.

Some Jefferson supporters have claimed that it was a romantic relationship. They said Jefferson loved Hemings. Others have pointed out that Hemings could not choose to be his lover or mistress. She was enslaved by him. No matter what she felt, she could not say no to her owner. Also, their relationship began when she was only 14.

It is true that Jefferson had some progressive views on slavery for the time. However, other founding fathers did more than Jefferson to advance the cause of ending slavery. Benjamin Franklin became a strong abolitionist later in life. George Washington freed all of his slaves in his will.

For all his talk about hating slavery, Jefferson did very little to end it in his personal life. Of the 607 enslaved people he owned, he freed only two of them while he was alive. He freed just five more after his death—children of Sally Hemings. But he never freed Sally herself.

An exhibit at the Smithsonian National Museum of African American History and Culture in Washington, D.C., featured bricks marked with the names of enslaved people who were held by Thomas Jefferson.

CHAPTER FIVE

JEFFERSON'S LASTING LEGACY

Every year on July 4, Americans celebrate their country's independence. But July 4 is not the day the Revolutionary War was won. It is not the day the country's Constitution was ratified or its first president was elected. July 4 is the day the Continental Congress adopted the Declaration of Independence. The war was still going on. The American colonies might have won independence. Or they might not have.

The meaning of this document is made clear by its title. It declared that Americans were independent from Great Britain. And it explained why. As the author of the Declaration, Thomas Jefferson stands at the center of America's beliefs. When people celebrate Independence Day, they remind themselves of the values he laid out for the country.

All people are equal. Everyone has rights. Everyone deserves freedom and opportunity.

Just days after the Declaration of Independence was signed, General George Washington read it to his troops in New York. They listened to the inspiring words about how all men were created equal. They all had the rights to life, liberty, and the pursuit of happiness. England had violated these rights. Because of that, the people of America had the right to break free from England's rule.

Jefferson's words moved and inspired the soldiers and citizens who heard them. People ran down Broadway toward a large statue of George III, the king of England. They knocked it over and cut off its head. Later, they melted down the body and made it into bullets. These they used to fight the British and help give birth to a new nation.

All his life, Jefferson fought for people's rights. He fought for people to have power, not government. And he fought for their right to education. That way they could be informed about how they governed themselves. Equally important, he fought for people's freedom to participate in whatever religion they chose.

Today, nearly all Americans look up to Thomas Jefferson. Conservatives appreciate his opposition to big government. They like his belief in individual freedom. Liberals are inspired by his support for education and religious freedom. They also like how he supported regular people over the rich and powerful.

Jefferson's legacy is complicated by his record on slavery. There is no dodging the moral issues raised by his enslavement of black people and his treatment of them. His ideas about American Indians also trouble many people today.

Still, Jefferson ranks as one of the most influential founding fathers of the United States. He was a symbol of hope for oppressed people everywhere. He believed in democracy—the idea that people can and should govern themselves. And he believed it would become the ideal form of government in the world. He never stopped believing it.

Thomas Jefferson died July 4, 1826. It was the 50th anniversary of the Declaration of Independence. He still believed in everything it stood for. Only a few days before he died, he said, "All eyes are opened, or opening, to the rights of man."

Through the centuries Americans have continued to look up to Jefferson. One story about another president helps to explain the depth of that admiration. In 1962, President John F. Kennedy invited a group of Nobel Prize winners to the White House. These are typically among the most intelligent and inspiring thinkers in the world. What did Kennedy say to this room full of brilliant people?

The 35th president said, "This is the most extraordinary collection of talent, of human knowledge, that has ever been gathered at the White House with the possible exception of when Thomas Jefferson dined alone."

Jefferson may have been imperfect in his perception of equality, but his contributions to the formation of the United States created a foundation upon which future Americans could strive for equality for all.

TIMELINE

1743

Thomas Jefferson is born in Virginia.

1762

Jefferson graduates from the College of William and Mary in Williamsburg, Virginia.

1767

Jefferson begins practicing law.

1769

Construction begins on Monticello, the house in Virginia that Jefferson designed and lived in most of his life.

1772

Jefferson marries Martha Wayles Skelton.

1776

As a delegate to the Continental Congress, Jefferson writes a first draft of the Declaration of Independence. After edits from others, Congress formally adopts the Declaration on July 4.

1779

Jefferson becomes governor of Virginia.

1783

Jefferson is elected to Congress.

1785

Jefferson is appointed minister to France.

1789

Jefferson is appointed secretary of state by President George Washington.

1796

Jefferson becomes U.S. vice president after coming in second to John Adams in the presidential election.

1801

Jefferson wins a vote in the U.S. House of Representatives to become the third U.S. president.

1803

President Jefferson signs the Louisiana Purchase, doubling the size of the United States.

1804

The Lewis and Clark expedition to map the unsettled western territory begins; Jefferson is reelected president.

1809

Jefferson completes his second term as president and returns to Monticello.

1819

Jefferson founds the University of Virginia.

1826

Jefferson dies at Monticello on July 4.

GLOSSARY

archaeology—the scientific study of past human life

architecture—the art and science of designing and building structures

artifact—an object used in the past that was made by people

construe—to interpret the meaning or intention of something

delegate—a representative of a U.S. territory to a conference

Democratic-Republican—a major American political party of the early 19th century that favored restricting the powers of the federal government and emphasizing states' rights

diplomat—a person who conducts negotiations between nations

economy—the way a country runs its industry, trade, and finance

excavate—to dig in the earth to search for ancient remains

Federalist—a member of a major political party in the early years of the U.S. favoring a strong centralized national government

hypocrite—a person whose actions are contrary to his or her stated beliefs

independence—freedom from the control of other people or things

monarchy—when a country is run by a single ruler such as a king or queen who has absolute power

recession—a time when business slows down, and more workers than usual are unemployed

tolerance—willingness to respect or accept the customs, beliefs, or opinions of others

treason—the crime of betraying one's country by spying for another country or by helping an enemy during war

FURTHER READING

Meacham, Jon. *Thomas Jefferson: President and Philosopher.* New York: Crown Books for Young Readers, 2014.

Thomas, Peggy. *Thomas Jefferson Grows a Nation.* Honesdale, PA.: Calkins Creek Publishers, 2015.

Roxburgh, Ellis. *Thomas Jefferson vs. John Adams: Founding Fathers and Political Rivals.* Milwaukee, WI: Gareth Stevens Publishing, 2016.

SOURCE NOTES

p. 9, "I am obnoxious..." John Adams, "Thomas Jefferson." https://www.loc.gov/collections/continental-congress-and-constitutional-convention-from-1774-to-1789/articles-and-essays/to-form-a-more-perfect-union/thomas-jefferson/ Accessed September 27, 2018.

p. 11, "It does me no injury..." Thomas Jefferson. *Notes on the State of Virginia.* http://xroads.virginia.edu/~hyper/jefferson/ch17.html Accessed September 27, 2018.

p. 14, "every falsehood..." Thomas Jefferson. "First Inauguration." https://www.monticello.org/site/research-and-collections/first-inauguration Accessed September 27, 2018.

p. 25, "I believe the Indian..." Thomas Jefferson. "American Indians." https://www.monticello.org/site/jefferson/american-indians Accessed September 27, 2018.

p. 26, "as incapable..." Thomas Jefferson. "Thomas Jefferson's Attitudes Toward Slavery." https://www.monticello.org/site/plantation-and-slavery/thomas-jeffersons-attitudes-toward-slavery Accessed September 27, 2018.

p. 40, "expressions which..." and p. 41, "lying in..." Thomas Jefferson. "Jefferson's Excavation of an Indian Burial Mound." https://www.monticello.org/site/research-and-collections/jeffersons-excavation-indian-burial-mound Accessed September 27, 2018.

p. 45, "We can buy..." Thomas Jefferson. "Jefferson, the Agronomist." https://www.varsitytutors.com/earlyamerica/jefferson-primer/agronomist Accessed September 27, 2018.

p. 50, "We have the wolf..." Thomas Jefferson. "Thomas Jefferson Biography." https://www.biography.com/people/thomas-jefferson-9353715 Accessed September 27, 2018.

p. 56, "All eyes..." Thomas Jefferson. "Thomas Jefferson, a Brief Biography." https://www.monticello.org/site/jefferson/thomas-jefferson-brief-biography Accessed September 27, 2018.

p. 56, "This is the most extraordinary..." John F. Kennedy. "Extract from John F. Kennedy's Remarks at Dinner Honoring Nobel Prize Winners of the Western Hemisphere. http://tjrs.monticello.org/letter/1856 Accessed September 27, 2018.

SELECT BIBLIOGRAPHY

"1778: Josiah Phillips, Attainted by Thomas Jefferson." executedtoday.com. http://www.executedtoday.com/2013/12/04/1778-josiah-phillips-attainted-by-thomas-jefferson/ Accessed September 27, 2018.

Bates, Karen Grigsby. "Life At Jefferson's Monticello, As His Slaves Saw It." NPR Weekend Edition Sunday, March 11, 2012. https://www.npr.org/2012/03/11/148305319/life-at-jeffersons-monticello-as-his-slaves-saw-it Accessed September 27, 2018. "Bill to Attaint Josiah Philips and Others, [28 May 1778]." Founders Online. https://founders.archives.gov/documents/Jefferson/01-02-02-0064 Accessed September 27, 2018.

"Building the Academical Village." National Park Service. https://www.nps.gov/nr/twhp/wwwlps/lessons/92uva/92facts2.htm Accessed September 27, 2018.

Danielle, Britni. "Sally Hemings Wasn't Thomas Jefferson's Mistress. She Was His Property." Washington Post, July 7, 2017. https://www.washingtonpost.com/outlook/sally-hemings-wasnt-thomas-jeffersons-mistress-she-was-his-property/2017/07/06/db5844d4-625d-11e7-8adc-fea80e32bf47_story.html?utm_term=.646be61406f7 Accessed September 27, 2018.

Edwards, Owen. "How Thomas Jefferson Created His Own Bible." Smithsonian Magazine, January 2012. https://www.smithsonianmag.com/arts-culture/how-thomas-jefferson-created-his-own-bible-5659505 Accessed September 27, 2018.

Freeman, Joanne B. "Jefferson and Hamilton, Political Rivals in Washington's Cabinet." mountvernon.org.https://www.mountvernon.org/george-washington/the-first-president/washingtons-presidential-cabinet/jefferson-and-hamilton-political-rivals/ Accessed September 27, 2018.

"Presidential Historians Survey 2017." C-SPAN. https://www.c-span.org/presidentsurvey2017/?personid=39786 Accessed September 27, 2018.

Richard N. Ostling. "Jefferson's Abridged Bible." Washington Post, August 25, 2001. https://www.washingtonpost.com/archive/local/2001/08/25/jeffersons-abridged-bible/e654d50d-17ed-474f-90b5-5f4e98ee4eb1/?noredirect=on&utm_term=.9845697208dd Accessed September 27, 2018.

This Is Monticello. www.monticello.org Accessed September 27, 2018.

"Thomas Jefferson Biography." Biography.com. https://www.biography.com/people/thomas-jefferson-9353715 Accessed September 27, 2018.

"Thomas Jefferson." University of Virginia Miller Center. https://millercenter.org/president/jefferson Accessed September 27, 2018.

INDEX